To Lewis, with love

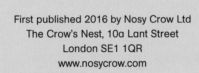

First published 2016 by Nosy Crow Ltd
The Crow's Nest, 10a Lant Street
London SE1 1QR
www.nosycrow.com

ISBN 978 0 85763 253 1 (HB)
ISBN 978 0 85763 558 7 (PB)

Nosy Crow and associated logos are trademarks
and/or registered trademarks of Nosy Crow Ltd.

Concept and story research by Barry Tranter and Emma Tranter
Text © Emma Tranter 2016
Illustrations © Barry Tranter 2016
Consultant: Chris Jarvis, Education Officer at the
Oxford University Museum of Natural History

The right of Emma Tranter to be identified as the author and Barry Tranter
to be identified as the illustrator of this work has been asserted.

A CIP catalogue record for this book is available from the British Library.

Printed in China by Imago

Papers used by Nosy Crow are made
from wood grown in sustainable forests.

1 3 5 7 9 8 6 4 2 (HB)
1 3 5 7 9 8 6 4 2 (PB)

Franklin Frog

Jump to it!

Barry Tranter  **Emma Tranter**

Meet Franklin. Franklin is a frog.
Here he is sitting on a lily pad in his pond.
Franklin loves being in and around water.

Different types of frog are found everywhere around the world except for Antarctica.

Most frogs are about the same size as your hand.

When Franklin is on land, he doesn't walk or crawl – he jumps instead. He can even cross the pond by jumping from one lily pad to the next.

Jumping is not the only way Franklin gets around – he swims too. His big, webbed feet push him through the water. It's a quick way to escape from danger. Look out for that heron, Franklin!

Frogs are eaten by lots of animals, including birds, badgers, otters and cats.

It's a great day for a swim!

Underwater, frogs breathe and drink through their skin.

Frogs can hide from herons underwater.

Some big birds like herons love to eat frogs.

Frogs can smell underwater better than they can see.

Franklin's feeling hungry now. He uses his long, sticky tongue to catch insects.

He's on the look-out for worms and snails, too!

Because frogs can't chew, they crush their food between their tongue and their eyeballs.

Frogs don't have necks, so they move their whole body in order to look around.

As the weather gets colder, Franklin must find a warm spot where he can hibernate for the winter. Hibernating is like having a long, deep sleep.

I'm off to bed. Now where shall I go?

Frogs often look for a pile of leaves to snuggle up in.

Because frogs can breathe underwater, some hibernate at the bottom of ponds.

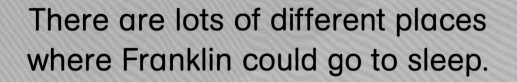

There are lots of different places where Franklin could go to sleep.

See you in springtime!

Frogs' hearts beat very slowly when they are hibernating.

Some frogs bury themselves in thick mud for the winter.

A sheltered cave is a great place for frogs to hibernate.

Franklin sleeps through the short, dark days and long, cold nights of winter.

And as the snow falls,
he remains safely hidden.

In spring, the days grow warmer and
Franklin wakes up. It's time to find a mate!

Hello, world!

But Franklin realises he's not the only frog looking for a mate! Lots of male frogs gather at night time and use special calls to attract females.

Frogs often return to the place where they were born to find a mate.

Frogs always meet in and around water to mate.

Some frogs' croaks can be heard up to one mile away!

To croak, frogs fill up their throats with air, then push it out again.

At last, Franklin's call works. Here comes Felicity!
She has travelled a very long way to be here.

Frogs start to mate when they are around two years old.

Hi there. I'm Franklin. What's your name?

During the mating season, frogs don't eat anything at all!

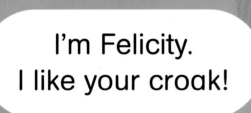

I'm Felicity.
I like your croak!

Most frogs
travel around
one mile to
reach a pond
and find
a mate.

As spring arrives, Felicity lays
hundreds of tiny eggs.

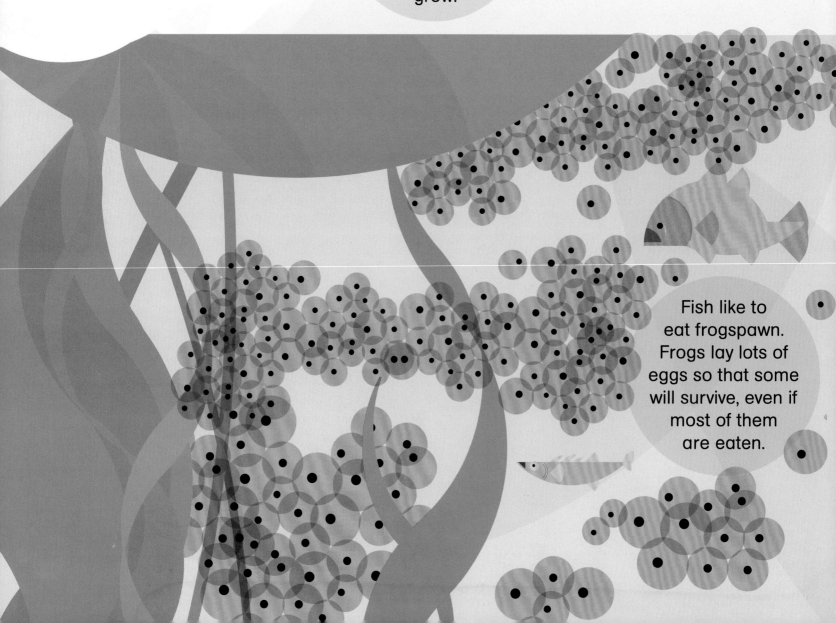

The frogs'
eggs float near
the surface of
the water where
the sun's warmth
helps them
grow.

Fish like to
eat frogspawn.
Frogs lay lots of
eggs so that some
will survive, even if
most of them
are eaten.

They are surrounded by a jelly which protects them. The eggs stick together in big clumps known as frogspawn.

Off I go!

Female frogs don't stay to look after their eggs.

Only about five out of 2,000 eggs will survive and become grown-up frogs.

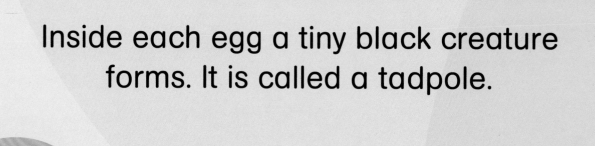

Inside each egg a tiny black creature forms. It is called a tadpole.

Tadpoles have gills, like fish, which means they can breathe in the water.

At first, tadpoles get food from inside their eggs.

Wow, I'm hatching!

After almost two weeks, the tadpole hatches and starts to swim around.

When they are four weeks old, tadpoles grow tiny teeth to grind their food.

I'm going to be a frog when I grow up!

Tadpoles mainly eat tiny plants called algae.

Throughout the spring, the tadpole changes shape.

About 10 weeks after hatching, the tadpole grows two big back legs.

When it is about 12 weeks old, the tadpole grows little arms.

The tadpole's colour slowly turns from black to greeny brown.

It slowly grows into a froglet,
and then into a frog.

Look – my tail
has disappeared.
I'm a frog!

At around
16 weeks old,
the grown-up
frog is ready
to leave the
pond.

After about
14 weeks, the
tadpole's tail
shrinks and it
becomes
a froglet.

Meet Fraser, Franklin's son. Fraser is a frog.
Here he is sitting on a lily pad in his pond.
Fraser loves being in and around water.

Hello, I'm Fraser.
Nice to meet you!

Frogs have
been around
for millions of
years – since
the time of the
dinosaurs!

Most
frogs live
for about
seven
years.

The life cycle of a frog

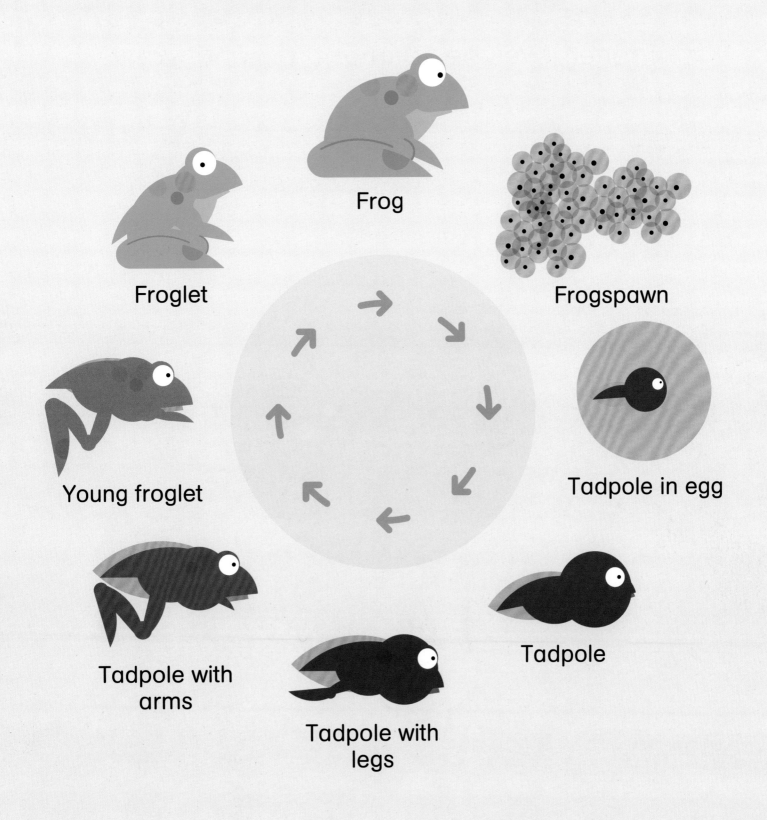